CLOSED COLLECTION

UNITY LIBRARY 8 ARCHIVES

C0-AWA-594

HAVE WE LIVED BEFORE?

By
Ernest C. Wilson

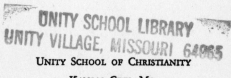

UNITY SCHOOL LIBRARY
UNITY VILLAGE, MISSOURI 64065

UNITY SCHOOL OF CHRISTIANITY

KANSAS CITY, MO.

1936

5/93

CLOSED
BL
515
.W5
1936

I DEDICATE THIS BOOK TO THE MANY FRIENDS
WHO WANTED ME TO WRITE IT

FOREWORD

THIS BOOK is not an attempt to convince any one of either the truth or the fallacy of the doctrine of reincarnation. Truth requires no defense, and error destroys itself. There is no value but rather harm in deluding ourselves or inhabiting a fool's paradise; but if the doctrine of reincarnation will help us we should know it, and should fearlessly and trustfully accept it as a part of our working philosophy of life.

The value of an acceptance of the doctrine of reincarnation, for the practical Christian student, is less in the remembrance of *who* we have been in the past than *that* we have been, and that we are and ever shall be. It assures us that life is continuous, that it is good and just.

One of the best reasons for believing in reincarnation is that in very many instances life as we see it is not complete. We sometimes see gentle, beautiful souls who have come into life under great physical handicaps. We see persons who undergo hardships that apparently cannot be explained on the ground that their negative thinking is responsible.

There is as much evidence for reincarnation, I believe, as for any universally acknowledged reality of being; surely as much as there is for life beyond death in the generally accepted meaning of the term death. But an acceptance of either doctrine does not depend primarily upon outward evidences. No amount of evidential experiences will convince any one who is not ready for the conviction.

When we are ready we shall be led into all that we need to know or can make useful. This volume may serve to make the connection between the doctrine and your own indwelling conviction.

There are many questions that any discussion of the subject of reincarnation is likely to leave unexplained in the minds of individual readers. This must be so, since we all are in different stages of development. To some the whole subject will come as a revelation; to others it will seem quite matter-of-fact, and to still others it may seem repellent. There are many questions, in any case, that your own common sense and study and prayer will answer; many that can be answered at least partially here, and our growth in wisdom will give added light upon them.

Uppermost in the writer's mind as he prepared this volume was the thought of Christ and His teachings. He prayed as he wrote that his words might bring comfort and light upon the path of earnest seekers for the truth about our eternal existence; and he has been encouraged by the response to the portion of this volume that appeared some time ago in *Weekly Unity,* and by the hundreds of letters expressing an interest in the question "Have we lived before?"

Ernest C. Wilson

Kansas City
November, 1936

CONTENTS

———

The figure of the Christ used in this book, drawn by
Willard Elliott, is adapted from a statue of the Christ, carved
in wood by Alois Lang, portrayer of the Christus in the Passion Play, and secured from him by the author at Oberammer-
gau, in Bavaria, Germany, in 1934.

HAVE WE LIVED BEFORE?

Evidences of Reincarnation

CHAPTER ONE

Truly there are persons and places and experiences with which we do not have to become acquainted. Somehow we already know them!

Chapter I

Evidences of Reincarnation

I hold that when a person dies
    His soul returns again to earth;
Arrayed in some new flesh-disguise
    Another mother gives him birth.
With sturdier limbs and brighter brain
The old soul takes the road again.

Such is my own belief and trust;
    This hand, this hand that holds the pen,
Has many a hundred times been dust
    And turned, as dust, to dust again;
These eyes of mine have blinked and shone
In Thebes, in Troy, in Babylon.

All that I rightly think or do,
    Or make, or spoil, or bless, or blast,

Is curse or blessing justly due
    For sloth or effort in the past.
My life's a statement of the sum
Of vice indulged, or overcome.

*   *   *

And as I wander on the roads
    I shall be helped and healed and blessed;
Dear words shall cheer and be as goads
    To urge to heights before unguessed.
My road shall be the road I made;
All that I gave shall be repaid.

So shall I fight, so shall I tread,
    In this long war beneath the stars;
So shall a glory wreathe my head,
    So shall I faint and show the scars,
Until this case, this clogging mold,
Be smithied all to kingly gold.

—A Creed; John Masefield.

AN AMERICAN musician on his first trip to Europe took special delight in traveling on foot from one village to another. On one occasion his surroundings became astonishingly familiar. "Surely I have been here before," he thought, although quite obviously he could not have been. He paused at the foot of a long, sloping hill, and had the amazing realization that he knew what was on the other side of it! Into his mind came a clear picture of the peaceful lake, the sleepy village beyond——

Eagerly he strode up the hillside. Beyond the summit stretched before him was the lake and the village of his mental vision!

During his travels this same musician, who was also something of a composer, had occasion to examine an obscure collection of old music. In the collection he found one of his own melodies, which had been composed and transcribed many years before he had, as he thought, created it!

The Boy Who Remembered

A lad of five, whose family's religious beliefs did not include reincarnation, maintained stoutly that he had lived on earth before and that his mother "used to be" his sister. His parents worried about the boy's "queer notions." For instance, they could not persuade him to eat meat. "Only very young souls do that," he would say. When there was any inharmony, quarreling, or dissension going on about him, he was utterly heartbroken. As Peter grew older he seemed to forget his "queer notions"; at least he no longer referred to them.

"Forgotten" Wisdom

A writer was attracted by a reference to a certain form of symbolism to which he found a vague allusion in a book he was reading. He was unable to get further information from the publishers or author and could find nothing in the reference works at his disposal; but the subject fascinated him. He describes the experience as being like trying to remember the name of some one whom you know well but whose name stubbornly refuses to come to mind. And the outcome of his interest was similar.

Half in annoyance at not being able to continue a chosen line of thought, he gave up and went about other pursuits, when, as he relates the experience, "like the sudden parting of clouds that lets the sunshine through, the clouds in my mind seemed to part and I found the information in my mind, awaiting my attention! It seemed to me as if I had always known it (although I had had no access to such knowledge) and there it was, spread out before my mind's eye, ready for use. Many of the ideas that I first found in my own mind I later discovered were common knowledge in that particular but to me normally unknown field. Some of these ideas however, though they seem as valid as the rest, I have never found in any one else's writings antedating my own committal of them to print."

The Child Who Came Back

Three children were born into a family. They were sturdy babies and very similar to one another in appearance. They were built a great deal alike and all were brunet in coloring. Then a fourth child was born, a girl, who lacked the sturdiness of the others. She was also lighter complexioned. And as time went on her development took a quite different course from that of the others. Whereas they had learned to talk very early, her speech seemed retarded. She had great difficulty in learning any words at all, and although her mind was very bright she had not learned to talk when at the age of four she passed on with spinal meningitis. Her physical disability and unusual beauty had particularly endeared her to her mother, who was inconsolable in her loss.

A year later another child was born, of the characteristic sturdy mold; but when two years after that a sixth child was born, she was so like the child who had died that her

21

mother declared, "My little girl has come back to me!" Moreover, as time passed she was discovered to have the same difficulty of speech. *But she did not die at the age of four!*

Gradually her speech improved, and she became a normal, healthy youngster, who has now grown to young womanhood. Although wholly unacquainted with the theory of reincarnation, the family accepted without question what appeared obvious to all, that the same soul came back again, on second trial overcame a physical handicap and retained a strong hold on physical life.

The Always-Known

Nearly every one has said of some new experience:

"I feel as if I had done this before," or of

some new acquaintance, "I feel as if I had always known you."

Truly there are persons and places and experiences with which we do not have to become acquainted. Somehow we already know them!

There are "natural-born" musicians and engineers and mechanics whose way seems to have been prepared before them; they seem merely to be accepting what they have already earned, whereas others have to study and labor so much harder to learn.

How shall we explain these things: experiences so common that the reader will find himself recalling similar and more striking ones? Are they not the indications of a profound truth that already presses against our consciousness for acceptance: the truth that life did not begin for us when we were born into the present life experience?

As this chapter is being prepared a strongly evidential story of rebirth is being published in many newspapers. The following press account was sent to the writer by a Unity reader:

"Speculations on the possibility of reincarnation have usually taken a vague form, and dealt in tenuous generalities with reappearances on earth of more or less famous persons of long ago in the body of some one of today who would seem insignificant but for mystic powers claimed on the basis of reappearing greatness. In India at present, however, a good deal of interest has been aroused by a curious case in which reincarnation is claimed without these accompaniments. Shanti Devi, a little Delhi girl nine years old, has, it is said, been telling her parents ever since she was first able to speak of having lived a life previous to her present one. The definiteness of the child's assertions, her application of them not to a far-off but to very recent time, and her seeming ability to identify persons with whom she says she lived in her former life, have aroused scientists, psychologists, and psychical researchers to regard the matter as one at least worthy of careful investigation.

"After she had recognized a visitor said to be unknown to her present parents as the younger cousin of her husband in her former life, relatives of the man she spoke of as her husband decided it was time for him to make a test. The story is that not a word was said to her of this plan; that he knocked on the door at Shanti Devi's home as a stranger and that at once she embraced him and cried: 'My husband has come back to me.'

"According to reports in newspapers in India, she has been subjected to searching cross-examination and found to answer assertions about her 'first' life in a way seemingly capable of verification—such as that she was first born in 1902, received the name of Ludgi, became the mother of a son in 1925, and that she died October 24, 1925, at Agra. These facts accorded with the experience of the man she claimed as husband. As the result of wide interest in the case and the decision of a meeting of ten thousand Delhi citizens she was taken to Muttra after it had been proved to the satisfaction of those proposing the test that as Shanti Devi she had never left Delhi. At the Muttra station, reports say, she identified in a large crowd her husband's brother, mother, and cousin, and addressed them in phrases common in Muttra but unknown in Delhi. Other similar things are cited as facts. The verdict of a committee of scientists on the case is awaited with interest, the Times, of Calcutta, says."

Thoughtless persons sometimes speak of babies as "little souls." Actually they mean little bodies, for the tenant souls cannot be measured by the size of the bodies that they wear but only by the measure of what they have brought into life with them. Many of the letters received from students interested in the preparation of this book, included accounts of children who remembered past life experiences.

Definition of Reincarnation

Although most of us willingly accept the

thought of pre-existence, many of us still object to the thought of reincarnation.

To begin with, we do not like the word. It has a kind of foreign flavor and is associated in our thought somehow with weird, Oriental cults and with the idea of being born again as an animal. Actually none of these objections is valid.

Reincarnation means simply the rebirth of the soul in another human body. The term is sometimes carelessly used in place of transmigration, which is the old Pythagorean theory of human re-embodiment in animal form. That theory has nothing to do with the Christian doctrine of reincarnation.

Reincarnation is no more an Oriental teaching than are the other teachings of Christ. Christ Himself, it must be remembered, was born in the Orient. His teachings include many of the truths already discovered by great teachers who came before Him.

Unanswered Questions

A truth is a truth whether we can explain it completely or not. A falsity is not made less false by even the most plausible of arguments. If the doctrine of reincarnation be true, it remains so regardless of our acceptance of the doctrine or the possible obscurity of its purposes or operation to individual human understanding. Whether any one of us does or does not accept it as true at any given time is of secondary importance. We shall continue to live and move and have our being. All that is true will remain true, all that is not true will still be false.

There are not many subjects upon which

all possible human questions are answered. In the scientific world there are widely different opinions and theories concerning generally accepted ideas. In the religious world there are innumerable cults and doctrines. All these diverse views are attempts to know and to apply the truth. There is probably some truth in most of them, and perhaps none of them expresses all the truth it seeks to explain. They are justified by the helpfulness they offer to humanity.

It is human nature to reject ideas for which we are not mentally and emotionally prepared. This tendency serves a good purpose inasmuch as it guards against overcredulity, but also sometimes it delays our acceptance of a new idea that could be helpfully incorporated into consciousness.

Open-Mindedness

The ideal Truth student is open-minded about new ideas. He does not grasp at every new idea that is presented to him, since he has learned from past experience that all are not founded upon Truth; but he is willing to consider all things, and to "hold fast that which is good" (I Thess. 5:21). He may find that he still has some prejudices, but he will not allow himself to be ruled by them. He is tolerant, open-minded, receptive to Truth, wherever and whenever he discerns it. His meditations and devotions help him to have clear discernment and understanding, to judge righteous judgment. He has nothing to fear, for he has no theories to defend. What is true is true, and he rejoices in it. What is untrue destroys itself and cannot harm him.

Worlds about us exist but dimly for us until something within us is quickened in appreciative response. When we direct our thoughtful and interested attention to the study of some subject new to us we are likely to be surprised at the wealth of information that other men have amassed concerning it.

The student of law finds a tremendous literature awaiting his attention. The student of design becomes aware of a world he little dreamed of, a world of thousands upon thousands of ingenious minds, busily planning and skillfully executing designs that add to the service and beauty of the myriad objects that surround us.

The Unity student coming, as he may say, "by chance" upon one of the Unity publications for the first time, having been previously unaware of any such movement as

32

Unity, is amazed to find that there are many millions of Unity students and readers throughout the world studying and applying the Unity teachings helpfully in the daily life.

So it is with the subject of reincarnation. Most of us have heard of it. Many of us have heard a great many mistaken ideas about it. Most of us, until we direct our thoughtful attention toward it, do not realize what helpfulness is embodied in the idea, what evidence there is for its truth, or what answers it offers for otherwise inexplicable facts of life.

Reincarnation and the Bible

CHAPTER TWO

I cannot believe that this little span of life is
all that God intends us to have.

Chapter II

Reincarnation and the Bible

I BELIEVE in reincarnation because something within me tells me that it is true.

I believe in it because I seem to remember that I have lived before.

I believe in it because of a number of experiences that I have had that I can explain in no other way.

I believe in it because of its logic. I cannot believe that this little span of life is all that God intends us to have.

I believe in reincarnation because there are certain situations that I seem to have met before and to recognize now as I approach them, even before I experience them.

I believe in it because every once in a

while I find something in my intercourse with people that is like the renewal of old contacts, the resumption of old friendships. Have you not had a friend with whom you never had to become acquainted, a friend that you knew the first time you ever saw him? Being with him was like resuming an interrupted association of the past, and you rejoiced that you had again contacted an old friend.

I believe in it because it does not contradict any other conviction that I have about life.

I believe in it, frankly, too because I hope that it is true. I want to believe that God gives us another chance, many more chances if need be, so that I can come and try this life again and do better than I am doing this time. The way I feel about this is as if I had worn out a precious garment and laid it aside and He should say: "Here, My child, I will give you a fresh new garment. You have another day, another opportunity. Go out from your Father's house into that strange country and do your best and be worthy of your sonship to Me. I will be with you, I shall not forsake you, and I will help you to express what in My heart I have always seen you to be. You shall declare in the world the glory that in the beginning you had with Me before the world was."

"But why is the doctrine of reincarnation not mentioned in the Bible?" earnest friends often ask me. The answer must be that it is. The direct allusions are not very numerous but they are unmistakable. For that matter, the references to the future life are surprisingly few in proportion to the great emphasis placed upon this doctrine by many churches and individual Christians.

An obvious reason why the doctrine of rebirth is not discussed at greater length in the Scriptures is that it was a very generally accepted doctrine (and still is) in most Oriental countries. We who so generally accept the Bible in this country forget that its origin was in the Orient. To Bible writers there was no point in emphasizing a doctrine that was already familiar. Allusions to it are casual and might even escape the average reader. When we become interested in any subject we observe its manifestations with greater interest and consequently with greater attention than others do.

There is, for example, the instance (Matt. 16:17) in which Jesus calls Simon Peter "Bar-Jonah" or, literally, "son of Jonah." The use of "son" here is figurative, implying that the present incarnation is the "son" or off-spring of the previous life. This explains the passage (Matt. 22:42) in which Jesus demands of the Pharisees, "What think ye of the Christ? whose son is he?" They answered, not as one might ordinarily expect, "The son of Joseph" but *"The son* of David." In other words He was the reincarnation of David.

In Revelation 5:5 Jesus is called "the Lion that is of the tribe of Judah, the Root of David." The name Jesus is the Aramaic form of the Hebrew name Joshua. In Revelation 22:16 Jesus says, "I Jesus . . . am the root [as Joshua] and the offspring [as Jesus] of David." Joshua and David are outstanding types of Christ, and in character seem to have forecast His coming.

Solomon, the wisest of men, apparently referred to the doctrine of reincarnation (I

41

Kings 3:7) when he said, "I am but a little child; I know not how to go out or come in."

Malachi (4:5) said, "Behold, I will send you Elijah the prophet before the great and terrible day of Jehovah come."

Jesus confirmed this prophecy when, speaking of John the Baptist (Matt. 11:14), He said, "And if ye are willing to receive *it,* this is Elijah, that is to come."

Again (Matt. 16:13), He asked the disciples, "Who do men say that the Son of man is?" The disciples answered, "Some *say* John the Baptist; some, Elijah; and others, Jeremiah, or one of the prophets." But Jesus was less interested in the man of time and sense than in the man of spirit.

Our Eternal Life

Could they, as He did, discern the spiritual

man who is destined to come into his heritage of life eternal beyond the sway of reincarnation? He persisted, "But who say ye that I am?"

For a moment at least the shadow of doubt and perplexity that seemed so often to rest upon Peter was dispelled, the light of understanding illumined his senses and he cried, "Thou art the Christ, the Son of the living God."

Our successive lives are of the growing, evolving man. Our eternal life is of the Christ man, whose "life is hid with Christ in God" (Col. 3:3).

Jesus dwelt on the plane of the Christ man. His consciousness was beyond that of time and space and growth. His was the vision of the perfect man dwelling in the finished kingdom.

43

He knew and taught that we are eternally that which in human sense we are trying to become.

He saw beyond the delays and postponements and gradual growth and evolution of life to the fulfillment of life. When others remarked that it was some time until the harvest, Jesus said that the harvest was ready then. Where others saw death and dissolution and delayed resurrection in the case of Lazarus, He beheld Lazarus in his heritage of eternal life; and because His vision was so clear He was able to call forth the manifestation of that vision in Lazarus.

Part of the message of Jesus was to reveal to His hearers that which lies for all of us beyond the realm of birth and death: the overcoming of death in eternal life. He nowhere denies the way by which men come

44

into that realization. When for instance the
disciples referred to the prophecy that Elijah
must come before "the Son of man be risen
from the dead," He said (Matt. 17:11),
"Elijah indeed cometh, and shall restore all
things; but I say unto you, that Elijah is come
already, and they knew him not, but did
unto him whatsoever they would. Even so
shall the Son of man also suffer of them.
Then understood the disciples that he spake
unto them of John the Baptist." Nothing
could be plainer than the acceptance of the
belief that John the Baptist was indeed the
reincarnation of Elijah.

Are We Born Equal?

Again, in John (9:2) the disciples, puz-
zled about the reason for a man's having been

born blind, asked, "Who sinned, this man, or his parents, that he should be born blind?" In other words, did he inherit his blindness as a result of the sins of his parents, or was his blindness the result of sins that he himself had committed in a former life? Jesus answered, obviously accepting both theories as reasonable but implying a different cause: "Neither did this man sin, nor his parents: but that the works of God shall be made manifest in him. We must work the works of him that sent me."

This passage again indicates one of the reasons why Jesus did not emphasize reincarnation:

He had come to show them the way out of that round of lives made necessary by their need to overcome death. He wished to show them how through Truth they could over-

*come the last enemy, death, and lift up the
body instead of giving it up.*

Jesus did not teach that reincarnation is
God's final plan for man. Neither does Unity.
Rather is reincarnation a token of God's love
for us whereby, if we lose the body, we may
be reclothed with another so that we may
try again to complete the great work that
the Father has given us to do. That work is
to exercise dominion through Him over mind,
body, and affairs.

In that question to Jesus concerning the
blind man the disciples raised a point that
then, even in a country where the doctrine of
reincarnation was well understood, troubled
the heart of those who worshiped God as a
God of love and justice. They could not understand why some men could be born blind,
or maimed, or otherwise handicapped when

others come into life under so much more favorable circumstances. Only on the theory that the present life is built up on causes established in past lives can we reconcile the inequalities of birth with faith in a just and merciful God.

Unfinished Thought

There are few problems more distressing to the human mind than the burden of unfinished thought. To be faced with problems, to be filled with questions for which we can find no solution or answer, is much more wearing upon our energy than the actual labor of working out a problem or supplying an answer where one is available.

Any thoughtful person sooner or later comes up against problems and questions that only the theory of reincarnation can answer. It seems obvious that all individuals in our contemporary world are not born equal. They are born into various environments, to differing stations in life, into bodies that differ greatly. Some have a more alert mind than others, some seem to be born to special capabilities, talents, or even genius. Some are born into bodies handicapped by deformity or disease. There are as many varying conditions of birth as there are individuals, and yet all of them are equally subject to the same laws of life. All learn the same fundamental lessons. All earn the conditions they attract. For obedience to these laws the same good results accrue; for disobedience there is the same reprimand. Is God then not a God of fairness and justice? Does He demand the same results from us all without giving us an equal start and an equal chance?

Justice

The rain falls on the just and on the unjust, the sun shines on black and white alike, water drowns or blesses black, white, Jew, Gentile, all equally. Is it fair that one race should have an advantage over another? that one nation should make another succumb to its rule? that one man must serve another and another be served? Have we not all an equal right to the joys and blessings of life? Are we not all created with that desire pressing within us? Is not the cry of Shylock, the Jew, in Shakespeare's play of old, the cry of all persecuted peoples everywhere? He said:

"Hath not a Jew eyes? hath not a Jew hands, organs, dimensions, senses, affections, passions? fed with the same food, hurt with the same weapons, subject to the same diseases, healed by the same means, warmed and cooled by the same winter and summer, as a Christian is? if you prick us, do we not bleed? if you tickle us, do we not laugh? if you poison us, do we not die? and if you wrong us, shall we not revenge?"

Everywhere in life we see that similar causes produce similar results, contributing factors being equal.

"Cause and effect, means and ends, seed and fruit, cannot be severed; for the effect already blooms in the cause, the end pre-exists in the means, the fruit in the seed," as Emerson said. We see that in the long run known causes or revealed causes are crowned with results characterized by justice. This is so general that any of us is inclined to look with dubiety upon a seeming contradiction to the rule; yet in the exigencies of birth it is contradicted. It is axiomatic that nothing just "happens," that everything "results," that cause and effect are unalterably related.

If then in one of the most important circumstances of existence this law seems to be denied, should we not believe rather that our observation is false or incomplete than that this law of life has failed?

The Answer: Reincarnation

Reincarnation provides an answer for these questions. It is based upon the argument that our life is essentially spiritual rather than physical; that we are a spiritual being inhabiting a body, not a physical being possessing a spirit. Spiritually we are born equal. We are all in exactly the same relationship to God. Variation in human circumstances implies varying human causes, and when these causes do not exist in the present life they must have their origin in pre-existence, for apparently all such results are not explainable on the theory of heredity.

No Respecter of Persons

If one has gone farther than another on the road of serenity, peace, and well-being it is because he *has gone that way.* All men may do so, and soon or late all men will. "God is no respecter of persons" (Acts 10: 34). If one transgresses the good law and thereby brings upon himself the sure reaction that men misname retribution, let none sneer at him. If we are stronger it may be by reason of past temptations and overcomings. He who yields to temptations that do not lure us may in some other regard have greater strength than we.

The Lessons of Life

Our life is like a term in school. In the grades we all are required to take about the same course of study. In high school we are allowed to select courses and major in those which we most want or need. In the university still greater freedom is allowed. The sensible university student will not look down upon the high-school pupil. *The lesson each is learning measures his experience rather than his capacity.* Sometimes an advanced student will voluntarily join humbler students for review or to take some course he missed and now desires. We cannot always be sure how immature or how advanced a student may be by reason of the lessons he is learning. We can only wisely say that he is learning that lesson. *How he learns the les-*

son is a better index to his development than what lesson he is learning.

Entering a classroom in some institution of learning whose students are of equal intelligence but of varying background, we might strive to estimate the worth of each one. One seems bright, one dull, one labors hard over his lessons, another prepares his with almost no effort. The dull one may be skillful in mechanics, or in athletics, or in art. In any of these subjects perhaps the brilliant student would be the dud. The student who is slow may retain what he learns better than the one who grasps a subject quickly—and as quickly forgets.

Our day at school may tell us but little of the reasons why the students react as they do. There is a drama or a comedy back of each one's enrollment perhaps. Equal though they may be in intelligence, they seem decidedly unequal in developed abilities along a given line, because of the intensity of their application, the way they have come, and the interests that have dominated them.

So with life itself. The doctrine of pre-existence reconciles the apparent inequalities of life with the universal law of justice. It may not be pleasant to suffer any limitations in life for which we can see no obvious explanation, but the limitations become much more tolerable and can be borne with greater optimism and assurance of divine justice, if we can see that the limitations may very well be the result of some path of life followed in the past. That in our own case we do not remember the steps along the way, the overcomings and shortcomings that characterized our course, is not very important. If it comes to that, we do not remember very much of what happened even so short a time ago as yesterday. *We do not so much need memories as we need a justifiable faith in divine law.* Having this, we can face any difficulty with poise and courage, because we know that just as every infraction of law brings its corresponding undesirable result, so every conformity to righteousness brings the corresponding good result. "Be not deceived; God is not mocked" (Gal. 6:7). *Every good thought and word and act brings its corresponding result with unhurrying accuracy and justice. "What we give out returns to us increased and multiplied."*

So much for the present results of past mistakes. But not all difficulties in which we find ourselves are due to past errors. Looking upon life as presented by the phenomena of

57

this physical plane, we see only part of the picture, only fragments of the eternal drama of the soul. A single circumstance, even an entire life, does not give us the complete story. It is like only one scene in a play.

"Yet I doubt not through the ages one in-
creasing purpose runs,
And the thoughts of men are widened with
the process of the suns."

Solomon sensed this truth when he said (Prov. 8:22-31):

"Jehovah possessed me in the beginning of
his way,
Before his works of old.
I was set up from everlasting, from the
beginning,
Before the earth was.
When there were no depths, I was brought
forth,

When there were no fountains abounding
    with water.

Before the mountains were settled,

Before the hills was I brought forth;

While as yet he had not made the earth, nor
    the fields,

Nor the beginning of the dust of the world.

When he established the heavens, I was
    there:

When he set a circle upon the face of the
    deep,

When he made firm the skies above,

When the fountains of the deep became
    strong,

When he gave to the sea its bound,

That the waters should not transgress his
    commandment,

When he marked out the foundations of
    the earth;

Then I was by him, *as* a master workman;
And I was daily *his* delight,
Rejoicing always before him,
Rejoicing in his habitable earth;
And my delight was with the sons of men."

Our Lives and Our Life

*With each degree of dawning spiritual con-
sciousness we are coming closer to that great
ultimate, the incarnation of Christ. We
would not be content with less than
that ... Our human incarnations
are steps along the way to the
great incarnation.*

Chapter III

Our Lives and Our Life

WE SHOULD not forget that reincarnation is not an ultimate any more than, for instance, going to school is an ultimate. You go to school to learn things that you need to know. Then you go out and use what you have learned. So with life. We keep on trying to live until at last we learn how, and then *we do it!*

As Charles Fillmore has written:

"When man loses his body by death, the law of expression works within him for reembodiment, and he takes advantage of the Adam method of generation to regain a body. Divine mercy permits this process in order that man may have further opportunity to demonstrate Christ life. But generation and death must give place to regeneration and eternal life. The necessity of rebirth must therefore pass away with all other make-shifts of the mortal man. It will have no place when men take advantage of the redeeming, regenerating life of Jesus Christ and quit dying.

"Through *'the light* [the indwelling Christ] which lighteth every man, coming into the world,' the so-called heathen have discerned many truths to which the more material-minded people of the newer countries have been blind. Whenever there has been a nation of thinkers who were not bound in materialism, those thinkers have accepted re-embodiment as a fact. It is rejected only where the craze for wealth and for fame and for the things of the world has darkened the mind with materiality."

Another Chance

In earthly incarnation man is striving to overcome his own weaknesses until finally he becomes the victor. "He that overcometh," said the Revelator, "I will make him a pillar in the temple of my God, and he shall go out thence no more" (Rev. 3:12).

Reincarnation is the gospel of the second chance. It is as if God were to say, "You have made mistakes and have lost the crown of your dominion, but I will give you another opportunity."

How many times we say, "Oh, if only I could live my life over again, I would do so differently!" Reincarnation is God's loving answer to that universal cry of the human heart, distressed by its own missing of the shining mark. Reincarnation is not a punishment; it is the mark of God's forgiving love; it is His gospel of compassionate love and understanding.

The evidence of this truth begins to have meaning for us only as we open our eyes to perceive it. With our vision focused upon the things of this world, many of us have been blind to the truth of our endless existence. But "the works of God" shall "be made manifest" in us, and through the realization of Truth we shall find freedom.

Again quoting Charles Fillmore:

"Some have thought that they could demonstrate eternal life by believing in the never-ending life, while holding to the idea of life's beginning. But nothing is eternal that has a beginning. So, if we would live forever, we must give up every limitation of mortal ignorance and say with Jesus, 'Before Abraham was . . . I am.' 'Glorify thou me with thine own self with the glory which I had with thee before the world was.' "

Spiritual Discernment

Literalists have a hard time in their study of spiritual things; for, as Paul said, spiritual things must be "spiritually discerned." The literalist says, "If reincarnation is true, where do we go when we die?" To try to answer him in terms of this world is like trying to describe what point in three-dimensional space the thought you are now thinking occupies, or how much in pounds and ounces a thought of love weighs.

In this present life where, for instance,

were we when, deep in thought, we were suddenly brought back to our surroundings by the voice of a friend? We were somewhere else than where, to human sense, we appeared to be. Where were we when, dozing off into slumber, we suddenly "came back" with a sickening jerk?

Are we not where our consciousness is? Is it not true that we are often much nearer to persons and places at a distance than to those literally close by? We are closer by reason of what we have in common with them. Dante was more truly in Florence than in any other place that to human sense he visited, because he so loved Florence (and Beatrice, who lived there!).

Where are you and I? We are where our thought is, where our interests and feelings are.

The Afterlife

Where shall we be in the life after this?
Where our greatest interests lie, where our
thoughts and feelings and inclinations take
us. How long shall we remain in that other
world? So long as our interest in and need
of it dominate us. We can easily imagine a
person who has lived a long and useful life
here on earth, welcoming an extended "va-
cation" from physical incarnation. Perhaps
most of his close friends have already
"slipped out." Changing times and conditions have made him feel less at home in
his profession than he did as a younger man,
a long and eventful life has been lived, his
thought and sentiments have begun to turn
backward toward the dead past, and he slips
into the invisible. It would be reasonable to

69

expect that he will "stay out" a long time.

On the other hand, imagine some circumstance taking a person into the beyond in the midst of a busy life of youthful activity. Perhaps he is just starting his career or is in the midst of creative activity. His thought is on the present and the future. He wants to finish projects that he has started, he is intensely interested in the people and things of the world about him. Is he not likely to seize the first favorable opportunity of re-entering the portals of birth, choosing, if he has earned a choice, such a parentage and such environment as will help him to have the experiences and the opportunities that his soul needs and desires?

Unfinished Work

"Why should a person slip out of his body

before his work is done?" asks a student. Perhaps the real purpose of his incarnation is served before his interest in earthly life has abated. Perhaps he came into the earth life not for himself alone but for others. Generally speaking, we seem to attract a life experience that is in keeping with our consciousness. "Whatsoever a man soweth, that shall he also reap" is Paul's statement of the law (Gal. 6:7). But it is obvious that this does not explain all human circumstance. We see great souls in humble and miserable surroundings. We see the righteous "cut down" in their youth or prime. Sometimes they undergo disabilities that are burdensome to them and to those who love them. "Why, why, why?" we cry out. It seems unjust. And yet we see that there is more in the law of incarnation than mere justice. There is also unselfish love, the unselfish love of God, who is "jealous" that we shall express all that He has envisioned us to be, and the unselfish love growing in our hearts as they respond to His own loving heart.

An acceptance of the law of justice, of cause and effect, as reaching beyond a single life span from birth to death, explains many of the apparent injustices and inequalities of life. Pre-existence alone affords a satisfying explanation of some of these circumstances. So often, judged by a single incarnation, a man's lot is better or worse than that which he would seem to deserve. By conceiving his lot as at least partly the result of causes set into operation in previous lives we obtain a possible and sensible explanation.

We can readily conceive too that there may be persons who follow some path of life that seems to us hard, not because they must but because by doing so they can minister to others. And they go their way rejoicing, for while in their human nature they may grieve for a time, their spiritual nature is glad and they find a deep inward peace that passes human understanding. Have you not seen such souls, standing steady and strong in the face of seemingly severe and even unjust persecutions, a light and inspiration to others? Have you not seen how some one's coming and the sudden passing has left a deep spiritual impress upon the family he visited? How those who had been completely engrossed in material things were made to see a great light, and to follow it?

Nor is spiritual growth simply a process of self-sacrifice. Spiritual growth does mean the sacrifice of our shortcomings and imperfections, our frailties and weaknesses; but such sacrifices are pure gain. We are often confused about this because, as Shelley said,

"Life, like a dome of many-colored glass,

Stains the white radiance of eternity."

We view circumstance through a glass that is colored by our human nature, and all that we humanly see is colored by that side of us. Because we are incarnate in a realm of three dimensions, we see everything in terms of these, rather than as they are in Truth and spirit.

From Sense to Spirit

To human sense the body, human relationships, and the environing world of sense seem all-important. We think of them, and appraise spiritual values as they affect the things of the world. Actually, while these are important to us since we are projected in consciousness among them, their importance is secondary to that of soul development. Instead of beginning with the soul, and considering things as related to it, we think backward!

We are souls. We have bodies.

We are learning to put first things first and bring all into right relationship. Jesus alluded to this truth when He said (Luke 12:18-23), "This will I do: I will pull down my barns, and build greater; and there will I bestow all my grain and my goods. And I will say to my soul, Soul, thou hast much goods laid up for many years; take thine ease, eat, drink, be merry. But God said unto him, Thou foolish one, this night is thy soul required of thee; and the things which thou hast prepared, whose shall they be? So is he that layeth up treasure for himself, and is not rich toward God. . . . Therefore I say unto you, Be not anxious for *your* life, what ye shall eat; nor yet for your body, what ye shall put on. For the life is more than the food, and the body than the raiment."

Our conquest of things and of self often seems slow to us, but even in that common fact we can find encouragement; for it indicates that we are actually creatures of eternity, not of time and sense and evolution. The true self of us knows that all things are possible now, that in Spirit there is no delay, no postponement, no separation. As we die to sense and are born to spirit we chafe against the appearance of these limitations.

It would help us to remember that we are incarnate on a plane of manifestation where we are learning to express progressively, that which we are eternally.

We are learning to sense and acclaim, successively, the wonders of God's world, which in Spirit exist simultaneously, in unity. We are to become consciously and progressively that which we are eternally in the mind of God.

"As in Adam all die, so also in Christ shall all be made alive," said Paul. "And as we have borne the image of the earthy, we shall also bear the image of the heavenly. . . . flesh and blood cannot inherit the kingdom of God; neither doth corruption inherit incorruption. Behold, I tell you a mystery: We all shall not all sleep, but we shall all be changed, in a moment, in the twinkling of an eye . . . But when this corruptible shall have put on incorruption, and this mortal shall have put on immortality, then shall come to

77

pass the saying that is written, Death is swallowed up in victory. O death, where is thy victory? O death, where is thy sting?" (I Cor. 15:22, 49-52, 54, 55.)

The story of man from Adam to Christ is the symbolical portrayal of this journey from sense to spirit. The fall of man, so-called, is his incarnation in human form.

At first he but feebly showed forth any evidence of his divine origin. His energies were focused upon the urgent demands of the physical plane. He saw at most one step ahead, and did not see the shining goal. Created to manifest the image and likeness of God and to have dominion over the things of the world, he yet bore in consciousness the stamp of the earth from which his body temple was evolved; and even yet man has not completely found his true dominion over himself or his environment.

Gradually he has been learning the lessons of self-discovery and self-conquest, dying to his Adam nature and being reborn more nearly to the nature of Christ.

So long as he trusted and obeyed God primitive man lacked for nothing. His every need was supplied. He was one with his companion, one with his supply, one with his God; he saw things as good; and he saw only the good. He was like a little child depending upon a loving and generous father, and his Edenic experience served a similar purpose.

Discontent may well have been the true name of that wily serpent who introduced him to the knowledge of good and evil; and bitter the fruits of that knowledge must have seemed to be. For they demanded growth, adjustment to ever-shifting standards of right and wrong until man should become consciously that which God in the beginning envisioned him to be. There was a certain wisdom in his discernment of good and evil, of God and the Adversary, and of other men as separate entities, but it was a half-wisdom bearing a bitter fruit of worldly and unhappy experience.

To see a power or a pleasure to be gained through overcoming evil, to see one's own good as separate from the good of another, to seek a physical satisfaction apart from its spiritual complement, is the deluding source of much woe. But it is the beginning of a deeper spiritual knowledge, tested in human life and leading to another, wiser Eden, the Eden of man's spiritual maturity—the kingdom of heaven!

God had given man a Garden of Eden, to

dress it and to keep it. His discontent and self-consciousness led him to dress himself instead and to lose the Garden. Assertion of his own will, at variance with God's will for him, has brought him many troubles and much pain, even death; but the remedy is not in a return to the Edenic state of no will but in the conformance of the human will to the divine purpose.

It is plain to be seen that the man formed of the dust of the ground but embryonically possessed the attributes of the man idea that God created in His own image, after His own likeness. There are many steps along the way from Adam to Christ, a way that goes through valleys of the shadow but leads to heights of radiant light.

The dust of earth still clung to Adam as he grew. Some of it still clings to us as we seek to find and express the Christ within us. Though sometimes conscious that God has implanted something divine in us, we are also conscious of a material inheritance.

There have been compensations for our choice of growth through experience however. We lost a garden, but we gained—or are gaining—a world. Unwilling to accept on faith the blessings and the will of the Father, we have followed the path of discovering consciously for ourselves the knowledge that His way is good, and that only His way is good. Experiment has unfailingly taught us the shortcomings and disadvantages of every other way.

Would we attempt some transgression of God's law and way for us? Pain, a faithful check upon transgression, stands on guard like the cherubim with the flaming sword to warn us to keep in the path of God's way until we shall have learned once again to trust and to obey Him.

The blind faith of the little child is, through various stages of doubt, becoming a wise and understanding faith. Perhaps after all the "fall" of man has been his salvation, as God intended; for why should He have made a wonderful world of conquest beyond the Garden unless He intended man to become the conqueror—and in the conquest to find himself.

In "this long war beneath the stars" we do not remember all the details of this experience in past ages by which we have arrived where we are in consciousness; but the consciousness itself is evidence that we "have come" into it. We do not remember, because the focus of our attention and interest has changed from the past to the present and the future. Our memory follows our directed attention, which is a clue to the way that people have in some instances awakened memories from the past. Such memory however, except in special instances, is unimportant.

It does not matter when you learned that fire burns. It suffices that you know it. The fact that you know it is evidence that somehow you learned it. You profit by the knowledge without having to recall, every time you apply that knowledge, just how you came by it.

You meet and master circumstance, and the very thing that seems to try your patience and bruise your feelings and your body becomes your strength. Edward Carpenter beautifully describes this truth in an allegory, "The Secret of Time and Satan,"

84

"And so at last I saw Satan appear before me—magnificent, fully formed.

Feet first, with shining limbs, he glanced down from above among the bushes,

And stood there erect, dark-skinned, with nostrils dilated with passion;

(In the burning intolerable sunlight he stood, and I in the shade of the bushes);

Fierce and scathing the effluence of his eyes, and scornful of dreams and dreamers (he touched a rock hard by and it split with a sound like thunder);

Fierce the magnetic influence of his dusky flesh; his great foot, well-formed, was planted firm in the sand—with spreading toes;

'Come out,' he said with a taunt. 'Art thou afraid to meet me?'

And I answered not, but sprang upon him and smote him;

85

And he smote me a thousand times, and brashed and scorched and slew me as with hands of flame;

And I was glad, for my body lay there dead; and I sprang upon him again with another body:

And he turned upon me, and smote me a thousand times and slew that body;

And I was glad and sprang upon him again with another body—

And with another and another and again another;

And the bodies which I took on yielded before him, and were like cinctures of flame upon me, but I flung them aside;

And the pains which I endured in one body were powers which I wielded in the next; and I grew in strength, till at last I stood before him complete, with a body like

86

his own and equal in might—exultant in pride and joy.

Then he ceased, and said, 'I love thee.'

And lo! his form changed, and he leaned backwards and drew me upon him,

And bore me up into the air, and floated me over the topmost trees and the ocean, and round the curve of the earth under the moon—

Till we stood again in Paradise."

The Great Incarnation

"But can I not complete my task now? Must I die and be born again and again?"

With each degree of dawning spiritual consciousness we are coming closer and closer to that great ultimate, the incarnation of Christ. We would not be content with less than that. The Spirit of God within us guards and protects us from that folly.

Our human incarnations are steps along the way to the great incarnation. Our preparation is the redemption of our world of body, mind, and soul, and spirit ("the city . . . foursquare"), the redemption that Jesus Christ exemplified to us in His victorious life. "I glorified thee on the earth, having accomplished the work which thou hast given me to do," He said (John 17:4). This we too are to do and are in the process of doing.

In the highest sense then reincarnation is a misnomer, for the true incarnation is the incarnation of the Christ. This we have not accomplished so far. "Man is not man as yet." But no effort is wasted. Day by day, hour by hour, moment by moment as we faithfully follow Him, we come closer to the great incarnation. "Him that overcometh will I make a pillar in the temple of my God, and he shall go no more out" of the body (Rev. 3:12; A. V.).

The Last Enemy

CHAPTER FOUR

*Death, Paul said, is the last enemy to be over-
come; but though death may be the last,
fear is the greatest; and through
overcoming fear we shall at
last overcome death
also.*

Chapter IV

The Last Enemy

THERE is, so we are told, only one fear, the fear of death. This fear assumes many guises, but remove its masks and you find that it is the same old fear.

Death, Paul said, is the last enemy to be overcome; but though death may be the last, fear is the greatest; and through overcoming fear we shall at last overcome death also.

We cannot live to our full capacity of joy and richness so long as the specter Fear of Death haunts the feast of our daily life. We are not living the overcoming life if we are living in the fear of death, or if we are living in fear at all. Fear is a paralyzing influence. Even in our dreams a clutching fear reduces us to helplessness. In our waking stage it hampers our achievements.

Should we then fear nothing? Do not many things rightly command our fearful awe? Yes, our awe, perhaps but not our fearful awe; our respect, unquestionably, but not our craven terror. There is that in us which is greater than anything that we may fear, greater even than death. When we find and gain confidence in that greater something, we shall respect power wherever we find it, but we shall do so without the abject terror of the craven. Through finding our inner power we shall overcome fear, and through our newly found courage we shall overcome the last enemy.

Perhaps we shall find too that death itself is not so much an enemy as is the fear of death; find that when we have slain fear we have thereby vanquished the enmity of death as well.

He Overcame Death

It is well to remember one Man who so thoroughly overcame the fear of death that He overcame death also and rose phoenixlike from the ashes of death. He quickened His broken body to new life, and uplifted it to so high a state of purity and so subtle a responsiveness to Spirit that it became invisible to the gross eyes of sense, and now can be seen only through the finer senses of the inner man.

If a man die, shall he be born again? Must we then surely die?

What can we believe of those that "sleep"? These are questions asked by every generation of men, and answered variously according to the understanding of those who ask. The answer is not to be found in the study of death. We shall never find the knowledge of life by dissecting dead bodies in search of it. We shall not find the immortal spirit of man in the tomb. We must seek the knowledge of life in life.

If a man die, shall he be born again? He not only shall be but he is!

Where is the infant that once you were? He became a child, you say. Where then is the child? He has become the youth. The youth? He has become the man. Which one of these persons, so different in thought, action, appearance, are you? You are the one with whom you identify yourself, are you not? When you were a child, you spoke as a child, you felt as a child, you thought as a child.

96

Now that you are full-grown, you have put
away childish things. (See I Cor. 13:11.)
You no longer speak, feel, or think in terms
of that child. You no longer identify yourself with him. You have become a man. Did
you have to die to become a man? Did you
have to die to become a child and a youth?
Do you have to die, perhaps, even to be born?
Yes, in a certain way you have died many
times and are likely to die many times more:
as often as you cease to identify yourself
with one form of expression and assume another. Paul said (I Cor. 15:31), "I die daily."

The Undying Self

The self of you that is observing these
changes, that persists in spite of them, does
not die. That self constantly seeks greater

expression, and each new expression works changes in outward form. You let go of certain limitations, you evolve more expansive ideas, and you clothe yourself with a form suited to those ideas. But whether you are clothed in the body of a babe, or a child, or a youth, or a man, you are you. You do not lose your identity even though you become identified with a different appearance.

You put on your wraps to go down town. When you return home you remove them. You are still the same individual. Were you wholly unclad even to the point of losing your body, you would still be the same individual and you would clothe yourself anew with a body that would express your evolving idea of yourself.

You cannot die in the sense of ceasing to be. You can die only in the sense of losing your body; and because you continue to live you will continue your progress from the point where you left off, and you will rear a new body, perhaps a finer one. You will continue to grow and to evolve and to change outwardly as you change inwardly. Eventually we believe you will have purified your mind, and also will have learned to purify your body, to such a degree that you will not need to relinquish it to corruption but be able to quicken it to spiritual expression as did Jesus the Christ.

Upliftment of the Body

To uplift the body into spiritual expression instead of relinquishing it to death and corruption may seem to us a far cry. It may even seem to be an impossible ideal. Granted that the evidence of failure to do it is abundant and that the claim of some persons to have duplicated the feat of the Christ in overcoming death, even though it may be warranted, would nevertheless be very difficult to prove. Stories come out of the East that tell of spiritually illumined men who have never seen death; men who have lived in the body for hundreds of years, and have then simply disappeared without leaving any trace of their bodies. These stories may be legendary; but if they are, they are nevertheless true to principle and are in that sense prophetic of what mankind shall yet attain.

The best authority for belief in survival after death is the persistent desire to live. Desire is prophetic of its own fulfillment.

Matter changes form, but it does not cease to exist. Apparently it cannot be destroyed.

We can assume (if we do not know) that this is no less true of that which animates matter.

The Purpose of Life

It is well for us to become satisfied, and then to dismiss the subject from our mind, and live. The purpose of existence is more important than the process. The purpose gives birth to the process, and that which produces is greater than that which is produced. The builder is greater than what he builds. The thinker is greater than his greatest thought. We are greater than what we think, what we build, what we express. The purpose of life is to express in even greater degree that which we eternally are. The truest and deepest joys we ever feel come to us when we are expressing our higher self; when we are meeting the challenges of life in a Christlike way. It is at such times that we capture some of the thrilling joy of the spirit in which God created us—the joy of dominion. And we are at the same time conscious of depths of being not yet evoked—the self of us that is without end or beginning, eternal!

That which you eternally are cannot be overcome by what it expresses or by what it fails to express. So long as it seems to be overcome, it has not yet fully found itself. So long as we are overcome by death we have not yet fully found our power.

Overcoming Our Enemies

As yet humanity is overcome not only by death but also by many other "enemies." Man is overcome by lack, by disease, by unhappiness. To overcome these enemies should be his first concern.

Let him satisfy himself that he eternally exists, that he cannot be annihilated by any of his enemies—even the last one—and he is prepared courageously to set about overcoming all his enemies.

They are his enemies only so long as he fears their mastery of him. When he learns to make them serve him, they cease to be enemies. Some one has said that weeds are simply plants out of place or for which no one has yet found a use. Perhaps all the noxious things of life are simply good things out of place or for which we have not yet found a constructive use.

Surely, until we shall have mastered the lesser enemies the last enemy is a kind of friend. If by mistaken thought and action our body temple has become pain-wracked and unclean past our present understanding to redeem, then how great is the mercy that provides that we may slip out of it and try again!

God's Plan for Man

God's plan for man is life: life eternal, life of body, mind, soul, and spirit harmoniously functioning as one; the city foursquare, the New Jerusalem of the Christ man. Any plan that fails to express this completeness fails to express perfection. For the most part man has not yet accepted this plan as an ideal, much less as a workable plan of life. He still sees himself separated from his ultimate good, separated from God, separated from others; and this sense of separation, when carried to its conclusion, separates him from his body, depriving him of a vehicle through which to express the life that is God's gift to him.

Man has identified himself with existence apart from his good. He has thus fallen short of the mark or goal of life, God's life. Another name for this falling short is sin, and "the wages of sin is death." How often we have heard that statement quoted! But do you know equally well the passage that follows it (Rom. 6:23): "but the free gift of God is eternal life in Christ Jesus"?

God's Free Gift

The free gift of God is eternal life! With that conviction securely established in our mind and heart, the attainment of that eternal life ceases to be the heavy burden that otherwise it might be. In the assurance of the life and power that we have within us, we find new inspiration, new courage, new strength and power. It is this message, more than any other, that Christ Jesus gave to the world.

What We Remember—
and What We Don't!

*God watches over all. By ways both obvious
and obscure His purposes are served, and
His divine and truly begotten Son
emerges in us, as from the beginning He planned and
intended.*

Chapter V

What We Remember--and What We Don't!

While sauntering through the crowded street,
Some half-remembered fact I meet,
Albeit upon no mortal shore
That face, methinks, has smiled before.
Lost in a gay and festal throng,
I tremble at some tender song—
Set to an air whose golden bars
I must have heard in other stars. . . .
At sunset, as I calmly stand,
A stranger on an alien strand—
Familiar as my childhood's home
Seems the long stretch of wave and foam.

> *—Pre-existence; Paul Hamilton Hayne.*

IN MANY a novel and drama the life and liberty of some person accused of crime depends upon his ability to remember and account for his whereabouts within certain hours of a certain day. In a motion picture current at the time this chapter is being written, such a situation hinges upon the answer to a question, "Where were you at five o'clock yesterday afternoon?" In another motion picture a man's guilt or innocence is made dependent upon his ability to describe the appearance of a witness. Was she dark or fair? Short or tall? What was the color of her clothing? Did she wear a hat? Was her coat short or long?

In a celebrated court trial of a few years ago the guilt or innocence of an accused man was to be judged by his ability to remember and to prove where he was at a certain hour two years before, and whether the sun was shining brightly or the sky was cloudy at the time. In another more recent case seven witnesses declared they positively remembered seeing a certain man at the scene of a crime. It was later proved beyond a doubt that he could not have been there at that time.

Some one asks us such a simple question as "How did you come to work this morning?" and we must stop to think just what route we followed. Even after due thought it is quite possible that we are mistaken.

Nothing Just Happens

Most of us live more truly in our purposes and achievements than we do in the world of things and circumstances. We consciously remember only a very small part of what hap-

111

pens to us in any day or week or year. We are in a certain place geographically, we are in a certain state of mind mentally and emotionally, we are in a condition of affluence or financial embarrassment. Obviously, since we are in these places and conditions, we must somehow have arrived at them. But to explain the successive steps of our arrival would baffle most of us. The woodsman may not be able to tell you when and how he learned each item of his wood lore, the writer may not be able to give you the rule that governs a certain form of speech, the mechanic cannot explain his peculiar "knack" for handling tools or working with metals, the schoolboy cannot explain how he estimates distance as he swings at a pitched ball.

Jesse Owens, the great colored track star, was asked to describe his broad-jump technique. "Well, I just go as far back as I should, run as fast as I think I ought to, jump as high as I can, and let results take care of themselves." In his case, they are very good! But none of these things "just happened." They "resulted." A special proficiency implies a special preparation or a special aptitude. And does not a special aptitude itself imply some special preparation by heredity, training, or through pre-existence? To possess an ability indicates that at some time we earned it.

What to Forget

To have to remember all that has happened to us and all that we have thought about during our lifetime would be an incalculable burden. It would leave no time for creative thought, hence prevent progress. Fortunately

most of the details of our daily experiences
sink beneath the level of our conscious
thought. Thereby our conscious mind is left
free to consider new possibilities, opportunities, and ideas.

"The moving finger writes; and, having writ,
  Moves on."

Our experiences are recorded as impres-
sions, feelings, and conclusions. We find that
as a result of past experiences we have certain conceptions of persons and places; that
we take one course of action and refrain from
another. We do not usually stop to analyze
all the contributing factors that lead to the
outcome. We remember the *lessons* of experience better than we do the experiences themselves; which undoubtedly is a very good
thing, and a thing that should be cultivated
beyond its present manifestation.

114

Particularly as regards unhappy experiences this tendency of the mind to progress from specific instances and incidents to general conclusions is a most merciful and helpful one. A too-specific memory of past discouragements and failures is a deterrent to present and future effort and consequent success.

Not to remember too many painful things from the past is a help, since it must be obvious to us that we have somehow got through the experiences in order to reach our present position, and it is therefore logical to think that if we have survived the problems of the past we shall survive those of the present also.

More important in a practical sense than remembrance of what we have been and have done in the past is the consideration of

115

what we shall do about the responsibilities
and opportunities of the present.

Effort of New Experience

New and strange mental experiences demand far more of our mental and even physical energies than do our accustomed activi-
ties. Driving an automobile for the first time,
for instance, was a conscious effort dangerous
alike to ourselves and to others. But with persistent and repeated trials at driving the man-
ual acts involved gradually sink beneath the
surface of our consciousness. We drive, as
we say, "automatically." We "instinctively"
avoid pedestrians, approaching cars, obstacles
along the way, ditches, ruts, and other
hazards.

It is not necessary, every time we employ

some useful knowledge, to recall the occasion of learning it. Sufficient is the fact that we *have* learned it, as evidenced in the ability to employ the knowledge helpfully. So it is with the accumulated wisdom of the more remote past.

Ever-present Clues

A modern principle of crime detection is that everything we do leaves some trace. Bits of pollen, dust, and other microscopic particles cling to our garments as we pass along a road or through a field. Their character reports their origin to the skilled observer.

In a celebrated criminal case the origin of a piece of pine board was traced not only to the actual forest from which it came, but thence to the mill, the lumber yard, and the purchaser. Traces of tobacco will be found in the garments, the skin, and the lungs of the smoker. Our habits of speech, our gestures, our manners, reveal our background. Our journey through life is marked by myriad hidden records of the way we have come. It is so in our mind, our consciousness.

Long after the remembrance of some instructive experience has faded from conscious thought, its results remain in consciousness.

The Aeolian Harp of Mind

Buried perhaps beneath a thousand other memories lies the explanation of these emotions that wax and wane. The winds of circumstance, playing upon the Aeolian harp of our mind, evoke melodies that are strangely

118

but truly familiar. They stir within us the feeling of some bygone experience to which the music was an accompaniment.

A whiff of perfume recalls the face and voice of some loved friend who used it. We may not know the name of the perfume or remember ever having been conscious of that person's using it, and yet our mind faithfully brings up the long-forgotten incidents of association. More often still the mental pictures thus aroused are vague and shadowy, and are more felt than seen, more of the heart than the mind, lingering like the fragrance of a departed presence, poignant with joy or sorrow, peace or unrest.

If we tried by effort of will to awaken such memories we should probably fail, for they seem to respond more to sensitiveness of feeling than to the sterner powers of mind.

119

They are, it seems, a by-product of man's effort to know the law and live the life. They cannot be forced or even wooed; but in seeking the kingdom and His righteousness they sometimes appear among the added things.

They come by grace instead of law. Grace, we are told, means "free gift." They are a kind of token or intimation of the larger life of Spirit in which our human, mortal life is held. They come to reassure us of the reality of spiritual things; to bless us as we climb and grow—if we discern in them a blessing.

Back of every effect is a cause, and that cause in itself is the effect of a finer cause that preceded it, as the wise philosopher Emerson has reminded us.

Admit this and the logic of past lives and the heritage of stored-up wisdom is inescapable. Each day we are blessed by a dozen items of knowledge whose origin we neither desire nor are able to ascertain. They are results. We have earned them. We can only be grateful that they exist beyond the apparent experiences that sired them.

We can gaze in admiration upon a pearl of great price, whose luster and beauty surpasses description. A sequence of thousands of circumstances links the precious jewel with its origin in some far-off sea. Interesting in themselves perhaps those circumstances would be; yet they are inconsequential compared to the lustrous gem they have combined to produce.

It is so with the soul of man. Through countless experiences of this present life, linked by invisible threads to the lives of thousands of others in the present world about us, reaching by still finer threads into

121

a vast and remote past of our own pre-existence, that which we are today and are becoming is infinitely more fascinating, more precious, and more wonderful than any single factor that has contributed to the result.

Past into Present into Future

Possibly they serve no more practical purpose than this. Surely from a matter-of-fact standpoint it is profitless to delve into the hidden deeps of mind for knowledge that has no bearing on the present. What is past is past, as circumstance. The past survives its time and reveals itself in the present through that intangible quality, personality. We are what we are by reason of what we have been: outlook, viewpoint, tendencies, individual and often unexplainable, are the final survival of what was remotely an experience, later a memory, and is now expressed as a trait of personality.

Where we are is more important than the route by which we traveled; and the direction we are traveling is even more important than where we are. The use we make of present opportunities is most important of all. As the past exists in the present, so will today exist in the tomorrows, first as memory, then as an unlabeled but nonetheless actual addition to our spiritual equipment. We cannot take the things and circumstances of life very far in our ongoing. We can only take—indeed cannot avoid taking with us what we garner from them.

Inspired right action today augments past worthy efforts and helps to wipe out past errors, as constructive physical exertion supports past exercise, counteracting physical abuses and building sturdy muscles and sinews. The physical exertion survives in us, not as physical exertion but as robust health. The past exists in us, not as a train of circumstances that must be continually recalled to mind but as *consciousness*.

What we have been in the past or what we will be in the future is not a prime consideration.

The use that we make of the opportunities of the present is all-important.

As we further our own spiritual well-being we help to redeem and wipe out past errors, and we prepare the way for a future that will be serene and happy.

With every rising of the sun
Think of your life as just begun.
The past has shrived and buried deep

All yesterdays—there let them sleep. . . .

Concern yourself with but today.
Woo it and teach it to obey,
Your wish and will. Since time began
Today has been the friend of man. . . .

You and today! a soul sublime
And the great pregnant hour of time.
With God between to bind the twain—
Go forth I say—attain—attain.
  —*You and Today; Ella Wheeler Wilcox.*

Unchanging Law

Law, order, sequence, rhythm, intelligence, patience, love, and wisdom beyond all human estimation are involved in the great drama of living. In all that our eyes behold we see the operation of a sure and certain

125

law. The past brings its fruitage into the present, and all things work together for good. The soul of all things is held in the sure and gentle clasp of the almighty hand of God.

"There's a divinity that shapes our ends,
  Rough-hew them how we will."

The divinity is now working in you, making you aware of a life that is larger, richer, fuller than the one that you live outwardly.

As you become aware of that larger life through your study of practical Christianity, you will find that that awareness not only extends beyond the physical confines of life as we observe it but that it reaches beyond time as we know it. Your sense of values and proportions will undergo changes.

You will find that you identify yourself somewhat less with outward things, names, places, position, and possessions, and more with the spiritual realities.

You will think of yourself not so much as Mary Jones or John Brown, so many years of age, with such and such family connections, and of such and such a place. You will know yourself to be all these things and more.

You will know yourself to be the son of God, ageless, birthless, deathless.

You will realize that you have always lived and always will live, and that birth and death are simply incidents in that larger life.

You will know what Jesus Christ meant when He said, "Before Abraham was born, I am."

You will know what Paul meant when he said, "The last enemy that shall be abolished is death."

You will understand why Jesus Christ permitted Himself to be crucified, and then demonstrated that even so He could requicken His body into life and take it with Him into the heavens. You will be unafraid of what life—or death either—can do to you.

You will know that there is no separation in Spirit; that you are identified with those you love, not by the name you bear in common with them nor by the body you wear, but by love itself.

It is reasonable to believe that many friendships are simply the renewal of old associations and that bonds of affection and common purpose are not severed by our passing into or out of the visible plane; also that many associations do not continue beyond a single lifetime because there is no enduring bond to sustain them.

Assurance

You will know that God has given you all the time that you need, all the strength and power and wisdom and understanding, to complete your demonstration of dominion.

You will reach beyond time, as indeed perhaps you have begun to do already. Occasionally you may reach ahead of the time rate of the material world and catch glimpses of things that are to be, and you will reach back of the time rate and review things that are past, back even beyond the portals of birth. But if you are truly wise—so wise that the Father can helpfully share His wisdom with you—you will not try to see either the future or the past. If such vision is vouchsafed you, you will be sensible about it; you will not let your imagination run away with you.

You will remember that such things as past and future are unimportant; that today and here are the important time and place, and that they offer you all you need, including faith to fulfill the good that a loving Father has prepared for you from the beginning of time.

God watches over all. By ways both obvious and obscure His purposes are served, and His divine and truly begotten Son emerges in us, as from the beginning He planned and intended.

Other Writings by the Same Author

Master Class Lessons, cloth binding...............$1.00
                 flexible binding............... 2.00

The Contemplation of Christ, stiff binding.... .50

The Song of Life, paper binding...................... .10

The Sunlit Way, German, cloth binding......... 1.00

How to Meet Bereavement (pamphlet)......... .05

The Unity Viewpoint (given free to any adult who is receiving a subscription for *Unity*, *Unity Daily Word*, *Weekly Unity*, *Progress*, or *Good Business* for the first time)

Unity School of Christianity
917 Tracy, Kansas City, Mo.

PRINTED IN U. S. A.

22C-15M-11-36